Linger in

Lisbon

FROM BELÉM TOWER TO THE TAGUS RIVER

A TRAVEL PHOTO ART BOOK

LAINE CUNNINGHAM

Linger in Lisbon

From Belém Tower to the Tagus River

A Travel Photo Art Book

Published by Sun Dogs Creations
Changing the World One Book at a Time
Print ISBN: 9781951389048

Cover Design by Angel Leya
Cover Photo by Elisa Michelet on Unsplash

Copyright © 2019 Laine Cunningham

All rights reserved. No part of this book may be reproduced in any form or by any means, electronic, mechanical, digital, photocopying or recording, except for the inclusion in a review, without permission in writing from the publisher.

THE TRAVEL PHOTO ART SERIES

Ruins of Rome I & II
Along the Via Appia
Garden City Garbatella
Ancients of Assisi I & II
Captivating Capri
Milan Cathedral
Treasures of Turin
Panoramas of Portugal
Linger in Lisbon
The Splendors of Sintra
Spectacles of Stepantsminda
Grandeur in the Republic of Georgia
Tableaus of Tbilisi
Original Old Tbilisi
Marvels of Mtskheta
Paragons of Prague
Hidden Prague
The Pillars of the Bohemian Paradise
Lidice Lives
Terezín and Theresienstadt
Flourishes of France
Portraits of Paris
Notre Dame Cathedral
The Beauty of Berlin

FONTAINEBLEAU

CAMPAIGN

CONNUBIAL

STYLIZED

TRADE ROUTE

GODDESSES

LIONFISH

HARVEST

BULLOCK

BEACH ACCESS

FLUX

GREENHOUSE

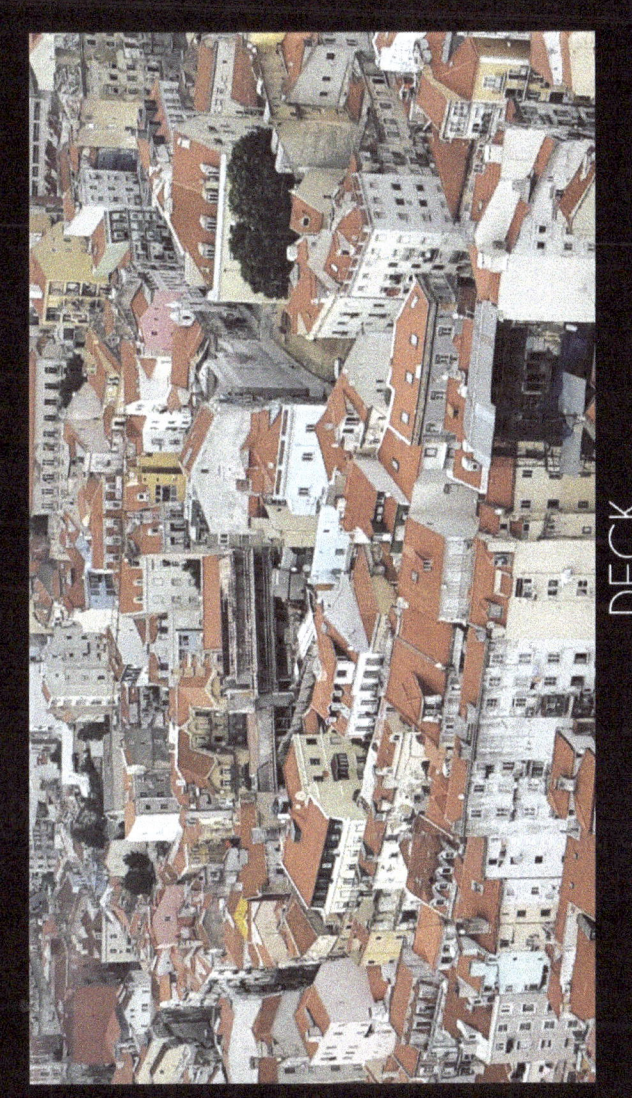

STREAMING

ICICLE

WENDIGO

ANECDOTAL

CORNERED

AROUND THE BEND

PROSPECT

PARKVIEW

SEVEN O'CLOCK

SAINT LOUIS

WALLACE

RAPIDS

About the Author

Laine Cunningham leads readers around the world. *The Family Made of Dust* is set in the Australian Outback, while *Reparation* is a novel of the American Great Plains. Her travel memoir *Woman Alone* appeals to fans of *Wild* and *Eat Pray Love*.

Novels by Laine Cunningham

The Family Made of Dust

Beloved

Reparation

Other Books by Laine Cunningham

Woman Alone: A Six-Month Journey Through the Australian Outback

On the Wallaby Track

Seven Sisters: Spiritual Messages from Aboriginal Australia

Writing While Female or Black or Gay

Ruins of Rome I & II
Along the Via Appia
Garden City Garbatella
Ancients of Assisi I & II
Captivating Capri
Milan Cathedral
Treasures of Turin
Panoramas of Portugal
Linger in Lisbon
The Splendors of Sintra
Spectacles of Stepantsminda
Grandeur in the Republic of Georgia
Tableaus of Tbilisi
Original Old Tbilisi
Marvels of Mtskheta
Paragons of Prague
Hidden Prague
The Pillars of the Bohemian Paradise
Lidice Lives
Terezín and Theresienstadt
Flourishes of France
Portraits of Paris
Notre Dame Cathedral
The Beauty of Berlin

The Zen of Travel
The Zen of Gardening
Zen in the Stable
The Zen of Chocolate
The Zen of Dogs

The Wisdom of Puppies
The Wisdom of Babies
The Wisdom of Weddings

The Beautiful Book of Questions
The Beautiful Book for Dream Seekers
The Beautiful Book for Rebels
The Beautiful Book for Women
The Beautiful Book for Lovers

www.ingramcontent.com/pod-product-compliance
Lightning Source LLC
Chambersburg PA
CBHW041320110526
44591CB00021B/2856